ISLAND THOUGHTS

Whispering Winds of Newfoundland

Best wishes!
D. V. Harbin

D. Vaughn Harbin

COPYRIGHT 2022

VAUGHN HARBIN

Vicdansar Press

59 North Main Street, Suite 1

Deer Lake, NL

A8A 1X1

*

Book Design & Editing:	Deborah J. Young
Co-Editor:	Nellie P. Strowbridge
Photographer:	Deborah J. Young
Print Excerpt	Victoria L. Kawaja

ISBN   978-0-9864736-1-6

DEDICATION

For my siblings:

D. Wayne Harbin

Victor W. Harbin

Derek L. Harbin

Charlene R. Van Maren

Joy L. Plourde

Albert A. R. Harbin

The raft of life has swept us far

From childhood's unencumbered bar,

Where in our innocence we played,

And but for time would fain have stayed.

— D.V.H

PREFACE

I suppose it is only natural that I should write poetry. My sister Joy does, my mother did, as did her mother, and her uncle, as well as her father's cousin, celebrated Newfoundland poet, Georgiana Cooper. My first clumsy attempt to write a poem was in November 1963. It was a childish effort to memorialize John F. Kennedy, the slain U.S. President. However, the ability to compose poetry did not really begin until the late 1970's, when I was a novice teacher in the seaside community of Ming's Bight, Newfoundland.

One evening, while searching in vain for an appropriate poem to use in a lesson, the thought occurred to me that I might try writing a poem myself. Just as suddenly as that thought had come, a poem seemed to tumble out of my head. I grabbed a pen and began to write. I had the sensation of chasing the poem with my pen. Another poem immediately followed, and then a third. Thereafter, I found myself writing poetry almost every day. Today, I have nearly 1,100 poems, and continue to write.

While I have had a number of poems published over the years in magazines, books and anthologies, this book is the first containing only my own work. It has been said that writers should write what they know. Having been born and raised on the Island of Newfoundland, I have chosen to include in this volume primarily poems about, or related in some way to that place. A more inspiring, beautiful, and mysterious location, I can hardly imagine!

Writing has proven to be a great pleasure for me; it has brought me joy, comfort, encouragement, and a sense of having shared the same with others who have read my poetry. I trust that all who read this small volume of poems will enjoy it, and take with them something that will brighten their day.

TABLE OF CONTENTS

ISLAND THOUGHTS

Happy the faces that wait for me
On a rugged island in the sea.
Blessings innumerable as the sand
On the beaches of Lumsden, Newfoundland.

How loving the hearts there by the sea,
As faithful as human hearts can be,
Friendships as strong as the rocks that stand
On the windswept barrens of Newfoundland.

Oh, how I long to see them once more,
In that home where eagles and seabirds soar
Over the fragrant evergreen strand,
That is the coast of Newfoundland!

WHITHER BUT HERE

Whither but to thy headland heights
Might I awandering go?
Whence but from thy cliffs might I
Plunge to emerald depths below?
When might baleen leviathans breech
But in thy summer's breaking day,
And diving, plumb oceanic vales,
While minkes frolic in the bay?

Where but in thy majestic fjords
Might teeming waters estuarine,
From saline sea and river, fresh,
Mingling thus, in marriage combine?
Nowhere might nature more cunningly weave
A fabric wherein each several strand
To human heart doth so strongly cleave
Than on the island of Newfoundland.

EARLY SUMMER

I am reminded of early summer,
And small "molasses-yielding" grasshoppers
In a field of tufted mounds,
Where school children played
In nineteen sixty-six,
In an island community,

Called Stephenville.
I am reminded of sweet scents,
Of white clover and sour-tasting sorrel,
As we played "Statues" in the yard,
And "True, Dare, Consequences,
Promise or Repeat",
With kids from all religions
Who lived on our street.

I am reminded of my youth,
And the carefree days that were,
When watermelons tasted sweeter,
And cars with Florida plates
Seemed painfully exotic,
In a small Newfoundland town,
Called Stephenville.

ISLAND OF MY BOYHOOD DREAMS

Wild is the westerly wind that blows
Where the orange blistered sea kelp grows,
And waves in underwater streams,
'Round the island of my boyhood dreams.

Sparse is the grass and coarse the sand,
Where the sweetest wild strawberries stand
Atop the shifting Black Bank Dunes,
'Neath summer's sun and myriad moons.

Gray are the rocks 'neath a turquoise sky,
Where starfish and blue-black clam shells lie
Listening to whales and the herring gull's screams,
'Round the island of my boyhood dreams.

MAN IN THE MOUNTAIN

The Mountain's face looks down today,
As it has for ages now.
Each passing car that wends its way
Beneath its shadowed brow,
Receives in turn the stoic stare
Of that form worn bleak and bare.
A joke of nature played by chance,
This face above the Devil's Dance,
Or another reminder from above,
That God yet looks on man with love?
Methinks the former well could be,
And yet the thought of Deity
Enthroned above such devilry,
Brings the truth home clearly, joke or no,
Where God is not, men cannot go.

RIVER ROMANCE

Deliciously sour is the sorrel that grows,
On the Humber's sunny banks;
Sweet, like honey, the bee-kissed blooms
Of its clover covered flanks.
Wild are the calls of the herring gulls
That glide o'er its glittering waves,
Sailing past rockslides and mountainous crags,
And darkly ominous caves.
Mysteriously silent is the swell,
As it steals past Shellbird Isle,
On its way from the lake, and the farmers' fields,
In the valley where it rests for a while.
As reticent and wild are the sons of the sea
Its island home has bred,
And as silent and sweet, the young maidens who greet
Them with kisses so pure, that to me,
The love that grows here where the North wind blows,
Seems as innocent as it is free!

THE HUMBER

The Humber wends its way along,
Through stony hills and lush green vales,
Past fertile farmlands neatly kept,
Beside tall stands of silver birch
Midst maple groves and alder guards,
Beneath whose branches mayflowers bloom;
And ever as it wends its way,
The logs drift on, and children play.

The river follows its chosen course,
While man-made highways rise nearby,
And overhead strong eagles watch
The field mice dart from rock to rock.
The riverbank meanders on
Past deepening cleft and gentle beach,
And ever as it wends its way,
The logs drift on, and children play.

It whirls a devilish dancing pool,
And tumbles past small Shellbird Isle.
Beneath the mountain's weathered face,
**It hurries to its destined place,
Under stout bridges on pillars strong,
Surging forward, moving on,
And ever as it wends its way,
The logs drift on, and children play.

The river slows its pace at times,
As if it, too, has need of rest,
Yet never fully stops its flow.
It has to move; it seems to know

That even it has rules to keep.
Through circling seasons life goes on,
And as the river wends its way,
The logs drift on, and children play.

TWILIGHT AT DEER LAKE

When into the sweet and silken shades
Of evening's lowering light,
Rich tones of heavenly velveted hue
Blend smoothly with delight,
When misty mountain's crowned mauve
Is kissed by petal pink,
And graying blues with turquoise strands
Watch the daylight sink,
The Humber washes down its banks,
And hopeful wavelets leave a wake,
As ravens call to caribou
On the shores of this Deer Lake.

POVERTY AND PLENTY

Though by the streams of the Humber I languish,
In solitudes cold, and in pale tattered clothes,
What though the wind mocks me, ignoring my wish
For a world long gone, and a joy that it loathes.

In my heart I have plenty, my needs are few,
My soul is enrobed in word garments of gold,
My plate is not empty, I have much to do,
For ten thousand poems lie within untold.

BRIDGING THE GAP

The Nicholsville Bridge will soon be gone,
Or so I've heard it said.
They'll tear down part; the rest will sink
Into the riverbed.
Something newer, stronger, plainer too,
Will likely take its place,
A new bridge able to bear the load,
And the traffic's faster pace.
I know it's been needed for some time;
It's just the way things go,
Yet, I'll miss the graceful curving spans
That arched above the Humber's flow,
Like the ribs of a giant humpback whale,
Or an ancient castle gate.
Yes, the Nicholsville Bridge will soon be gone,
Or so I've heard it said

THE WINTER WINDS OF WHITE BAY

The winter winds of White Bay
Blow tenaciously tonight,
Determined not to be chased away
By spring without a fight!
With icy blasts of blinding glit,
They stubbornly assay,
In chilling sheets that will not quit,
To freeze the entire bay;
While in their homes the people sit
'Round the wood stoves' searing heat,
With lamps all ready to be lit,
If the power lines are beat.

IMAGES OF EMBREE

The soothing warmth of comforters,
Soft eiderdown in satin,
Wide black skies and twinkling stars,
And two-toned Pontiac cars,
The pantry with its yellow pump,
The chicken coop in the big back yard,
Roaming horses in the morn,

White sheep, newly shorn,
Lobster pots in fishing boats,
And red-faced fishermen,
Seaweed, squid, and the capelin runs,
Beaches abundant with sculptured rocks,
Blueberry bushes and poison plums,
Virgin forests, deep blue bays,
Puddings with sauce on special days,
Elderly couples with canes and lace,
Who every Sunday took their place,

The small white church my granddad built
With the stained glass window in the front,
Its hard plank pews that numbing felt,
The altar where so many knelt,
The study in the Parsonage,
Black Bibles limp with use and age,
Whispered prayers at mother's knee,
On childhood visits to Embree.

Until Harbin was nine years of age, his family often
spent holidays and long vacations that sometimes
extended for months in the parsonage in Embree. His
grandfather, Pastor Ralph Laite served the Pentecostal
Church there from 1948 to 1964.

THE SKIES OF MING'S BIGHT

Carefree seem the mooded skies of Ming's,
Whose images are borne on cotton wings;
Heedless as the shifting shades of green,
Within the dim and recessed forest glade,
That blithely change from emerald to jade,
Nor evermore repeat what once was seen.
Be not deceived by these that seem so free;
All things are not as they appear to be.

The ever-moving current of blue air,
Whose variegated faces look so fair,
That seems so independently astir
And free from any force that might deter,
Must nature's laws obey, even as I
Am only free whilst heaven's flag I fly!

MORNING AT MING'S BIGHT

From the wharf, to the bottom, to the other side,
The waters of Ming's Bight swell with the tide.
The dories and punts with their fishing gear,
Are moored and ready at every pier.
On cold damp mornings when the fog rolls in,
When the mists are thick and the daylight thin,
The waiting boats lie side by side,
As the waters of Ming's Bight swell with the tide.

HORSE ISLANDS

Daily from my rooms I see,
Two fair islands, strong and free,
Standing ever placidly,
Amid a steel-gray northern sea.
Once inhabited, now forlorn;
All human fondness from them torn,
They long have watched from far away,
The seaside town by night and day,
And oft' times envied with a will,
The shores for which men left them still.

A THOUSAND FACES

A thousand faces has the sea,
That bows her head at Neptune's knee
As she glides by the coast of Newfoundland,
From Cape La Hune to Fleur de Lys.
And I, mere mortal, but a few may see
As she lifts her grown and sweeps past me.

In the wake of her waves as she passes by,
The faces of those she has kept I descry,
The faces of friends far too young to die,
Whose forms 'neath the mossy sod now lie,
And faces of widows who yet weep and cry,
And faces of friends, like me, who sigh.

Yes, a thousand faces has the sea,
As she bows her head at Neptune's knee,
And glides past the shores of Newfoundland,

From Cape La Hune to Fleur de Lys.
And I, mere mortal, shall always see
Faces that meant the world to me!

EXPLOITS VALLEY

Thou valley of zephyrs mild and good,
Where once the gentle Beothuk stood,
Thy verdant slopes in misted shroud,
With vernal goodnesses endowed,
Ever entice, entrance and enthrall,
Till under thy enchantments fall
All men who heed thy whispered call.
And those once yours desiring to keep,
Thou call'st them back with time to sleep,
Beneath thy hills in shadows deep.

THE CABIN NEAR EMBREE

My grandfather built a cabin near Embree,
Somewhere around nineteen sixty-three.
It wasn't far from the little church where
He stood in the pulpit each Sunday to share
The word of God with his much loved flock,
And just a little farther from Fox's Dock,
Where baptismal services sometimes took place,
And at the other times, the great capelin chase!

The cabin stood on five acres beside Troake's Cove,
And leading to the cabin a long path wove
Through a forest of pungent spruce and fir trees,
Interspersed with ferns and cracker berries
That lined the path and its mossy bed
With snowy blossoms and Chinese red.

The path meandered over hillocks with twisting roots
That tripped small boys in black sneaker boots,
And often through branches of a scraggly tree
Gave a glimpse of the cove and the open sea.
We swam in salt water and in meadows ran free,
At my grandfather's cabin near Embree!

NOTRE DAME BAY

Where fronded leaves of deep wood ferns
Midst wild rose bushes grow,
Notre Dame Bay's shoreline turns;
Its soft sea breezes blow.
And to their ocean graves,
Wild rivers swiftly flow.

TWILLINGATE ICEBERG

Mountain of majesty,
Born in the sea,
How came you so far
From your home here to me?
You've come from the winter
To herald the spring,
Like a great floating palace,
In search of a king.
The seagulls consult
With each other, it seems,
As if they could drive you
Away with their screams,
But you in tranquility
Drift leisurely by,
In harmony one
With earth, sea and sky.

BY LITTLE HARBOUR BEACH

Just yesterday I drove
By Little Harbour Beach,
To take a few quick shots
Of an iceberg tall and white.

A young man stood nearby,
Just under a rocky knoll,
Preparing to paint the gunwales,
On a small white fishing boat.

I stopped with my camera ready.
He turned when he saw me and said,
"She's a beautiful sight indeed."
And gave me an outport smile,
All-accepting, open and broad.

"Aye, indeed; it sure is", I replied,
As I took my first photo shot,

Then settled in for a short chat,
Now that Colin and I had met.
He gave me directions to find
Another good viewing point,
And shook my hand as I left,

Feeling sure we would meet again.
I made my way to the viewpoint,
That Colin had pointed out,
Past juniper shrubs and flowers,
And sudden silent pools
Left there by long vanished waves,
Breaking over smooth, flat rocks.

A little girl tagged along,
Sabrina Smith was her name.
She insisted we should be friends.
"You're not a stranger," she said.

When I had finished my photos,
I got back into my car,
And thought as I headed homeward,
Where else but here in Newfoundland,
Are folks so accepting and open,
And friendship and smiles so free?

LANDFALL AT BONAVISTA

Out of the fog, the ocean's shroud,
The vessel's prow in pulse-like thrusts
Through transparent blood,
Moves toward the rock-toothed shore.
Each wave pump pushes it closer,
Then allows a brief reprieve,
As if the sea itself is unsure, or unwilling,
To commit the ship to this new land.
It seems reluctant to call this barren coast,
With its splintered stones and spruce stump guards,
The culmination of a quest, the dubious crowning glory
Of this Voyage of Discovery.

Yet, as though propelled by forces
Greater than nature's mindless swells,
The ship inches on until the rasping stones
Beneath its weary hull sound an unfamiliar greeting,
And the answering splash from the first sailor's feet
Makes the landfall complete.

SERENITY

She sought a quiet place,
A scene apart
From activity's taxing pace,
And found sunset serenity
On placid Mundy Pond,
Where a silent gliding swan
Inspired her to write
Words of encouragement,
Lines of living light,
Illuminating faith and hope
For others, weary of the fight;
Till, in her printed words, her art,
For many a tired, fainting heart,
Whose spirit would respond,
She, herself, became that swan,
On placid Mundy Pond.

Harbin's good friend, Deborah Collins, inspired the poem, Serenity, written on July 5, 2020. Collins is a former Newfoundland radio and television reporter, show host, arts and culture correspondent. She is retired now and uses her creative skills as an accomplished writer of inspirational Internet posts near Mundy Pond.

AVALON BARRENS

Should the people of this Isle, with voices endowed,
Refuse to praise their King,
The rocks on the Barrens would cry aloud,
And every stone would sing!

CABOT TOWER, SIGNAL HILL

The tower on the hill stands gaunt and gray,
Somber and silent by night and day,
Lashed by the fury of many a gale,
Sung to by naught but the seagull's wail.
Haven of safety and signal desired,
Historical site where Marconi wired,
Survivor of wars which around her have raged,
She stands, a bulwark of power engaged!

Mid rock, and wind, and sea and sky,
She rules this hill with eagle eye
Aloof from those who come to stare,
She reserves some tales she will not share.
Caressed by the warmth of a southern breeze,
Those who would know her must come on their knees.
Lulling them into an enchanted trance,
She fades illusively into romance.

ROCK-STREWN ISLE

England's mists roll soft as down,
Veiling ancient Roman town;
The Englishman holds this as his,
But a rock-strewn isle my birthright is.

Spanish vineyards flow with wine,
As hills in siesta rest supine;
The Spaniard boasts a land so fine,
But a rock-strewn isle, I count as mine.

Home of strong-willed fisher folk,
Land the valiant Norsemen woke,
Wind worn and barren, though it be,
The rock-strewn isle is home to me!

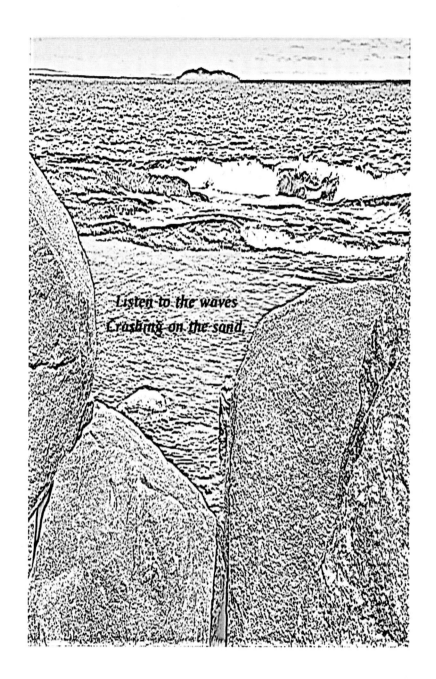

Listen to the waves
Crashing on the sand.

MAY IN NEWFOUNDLAND

Clear penetrating rains that seep
Into the rocky soil, deep,
That cause the slumbering Isle to wake,
And from each glacial crevice shake
Last traces of its winter sleep.
Faint rays of sun through filtering cloud,
Reflected from great icebergs, proud,
Give majestic grandeur to the sea,
While in the shoreline's leafing tree,
The wind through branches speaks aloud
Of approaching summer's warmth avowed.

ICEBERGS OFF NEWFOUNDLAND

'Tis spring, and in the northern bay,
The regal bergs in grand display
Guard the coastline faithfully.
Strong sentinels by night and day,
Their uniforms at midnight white,
And purest blue in stark daylight,
Are ever changing with their forms,
As spring's cool days to summer's warm.

SHOULD I FORGET

I know these waves, these hills, this land,
Its forests, and its coarse gray sand.
It is the land my fathers loved,
This rock on which I stand,
I know so many glens and dales,
And rugged coastline miles.
I've explored its many bays and coves,
Its inlets and its isles,
I recognize each strong-branched tree,
That waves at me and smiles.
If ever I should dare forget,
Or fail to love this place,
Let my worthless name be never found,
My passing leave no trace.

SIMPLE PLEASURES

Verse 1

As you travel to that far Eastern shore,
Where the weary nomad roams no more,
Pause as you pass Terra Nova's Isle,
To enjoy life's simple pleasures awhile.
To enjoy life's simple pleasures awhile.

Chorus:

Taste the sour sallies and pineapple weed,
Do it in the shimmering summer sun.
Young love never scorn, nor small joys shun,
Life's simple pleasures are all that you need!

Verse 2

Learn the flavour of the jaunty wild rose,
Admire the red cardinal's pose.
Enjoy the purple-petalled clover blooms,
Explore the fir forest's fragrant rooms.

Chorus

Taste the sour sallies and pineapple weed,
Do it in the shimmering summer sun.
Young love never scorn, nor small joys shun,
Life's simple pleasures are all that you need!

Verse 3
Listen to the waves crashing on the sand,
Caress the lamb's ears gently with your hand.
Watch irises nod and bluebells blow,
Relax and let your troubles all go!

Chorus
Taste the sour sallies and pineapple weed,
Do it in the shimmering summer sun.
Young love never scorn, nor small joys shun,
Life's simple pleasures are all that you need*!*

Verse 4
Skip small stones on a pond with a friend
Follow the alder-lined path to its end.
Lie on the moss and watch clouds drifting by,
Life's simple pleasures no money can buy.

Chorus
Taste the sour sallies and pineapple weed,
Do it in the shimmering summer sun.
Young love never scorn, nor small joys shun,
Life's simple pleasures are all that you need!

Verse 5
There's no other place under God's sky
Like Terra Nova for hearts that sigh,
And no better place to feel young once more
Than here on the banks of Newfoundland's shore.

DRAWN

I am drawn again
To the sweet-scented hills,
Where the purple bell flowers
Lie in half-hidden glens;
To the fern-lined trail
Where the grouse chicks flail
Their wings in deep, shaded bowers.

I am drawn again
To the mountains of mist
With their foothills of shale
Running down to the bay;
To the beaches of stone
Where ocean winds moan,
And the puffin sings to the whale.

DRIFTING YET TETHERED

Drifting out from the dock,
So secure, so serene, so safe,
Little by little, drifting out,
Till the whitecaps appear,
And begin their relentless
Slapping, chopping, tossing.
Drifting out till the dock,
So secure, so serene, so safe,
All but forgotten seems so far,
Till the rope stretches taut,
And the shore is remembered,
Straining, pulling, drawing
The drifting but still tethered bark
Back home to its haven of rest.

WALKING THE HILLS

Such exciting and beautiful vistas
As I have lately seen,
Walking in deep blue sunlight,
Over low hills of green!
The valley below me is gentle,
The river is winding away,
To what other land it is destined,
I cannot and will not say.
Enough that it honours this valley,
Enough that I hear it today,
The blessing its music's bestowing,
Is a debt I could never repay.
To walk here among the bog laurel,
To stand where the tamaracks bend,
I'll listen to the loon's lonesome call,
Then my voice to thwind I will lend.
And the wind will answer my singing,
And tell me of places it's been,
Describing vistas still lovelier
Than those I have lately seen.

NEWFOUNDLAND VIGNETTE

The snowflakes drift toward the earth,
Softening the winter night,
As an old barn owl beats the air
In his cumbersome homeward flight;
Soon all the shapes of the countryside
Will take on gentler lines,
As the snowflakes feather themselves down,
To alight on spruce and pines.

THE WANDERER

I have walked the heaths and moors
Of a coarse and rugged isle;
I have wrestled with the wind,
And felt the warm sun's smile;
I have kissed the pale moon's brow
On a silent summer night;
I have sensed the ocean's depth,
And braved the mountain's height.

And ever as I've wandered
Through the rich fir-scented glens,
Or clambered over the barrens,
Or struggled through damp fens,
The feeling life has brought me,
Has been peace and joy full-grown,
And the wonder of exploring,
Charting each new day's unknown.

WINTER WIND

Shake, shake, bend and twist!
Whence is the winter's windy mist?
Comes it from over yon distant hills,
Whence came the tuner of silvern rills,
When summer spread her tender hand,
And Terra Nova voices sang?
Shake, shake, bend and twist!
And whence is the winter's windy mist?

LAND OF INNOCENCE

Back to the hills of Newfoundland,
Back to the saline bay,
To the earth's last land of innocence,
I will carry you back someday.

And the whispering winds will say, "Welcome,"
As the breakers reach for the shore,
Where the bluebells and buttercups curtsy,
I will carry my lover once more.

Back to the isle of our childhood,
Back to the poet's lost lay,
To the meadows where seagulls keep vigil,
I will carry you homeward someday.

And the whispering winds will say, "Welcome,"
As the breakers reach for the shore,
Where the bluebells and buttercups curtsy,
I will carry my lover, someday.

Back to the wild rugged coastline,
Where the laurel and rosemary sway,
To the moorlands where young love once flourished,
I will carry you home, Love, someday.

WHISPERING WINDS

The whispering winds of my island home
Were among the first voices I heard.
They were the first to welcome me here;
Their song my first lullaby.

They carried the voice of my childish play
Over these barren moors,
And swelled the sails of my paper boats,
As they sailed past boyhood's shores.

And as a man I trusted them, too,
Though at times their griefs seemed sore;
Yet, the constancy that they gave to me,
Served to soften the frowns they wore.
When my vessel has made its final run,
O'er life's wildly tossing foam,
May the voices that call me from this world,
Be the whispering winds of my island home.

And the whispering winds will say, "Welcome,"
As the breakers reach for the shore,
Where the bluebells and buttercups curtsy,
I will carry my lover once more.

THISTLEDOWN

Blow softly the winds
That move through this yard;
Disturb not the dwelling
Where angels stand guard.
Blow sweet-scented breezes
Through the fisherfolk town,
Where nestles the cottage,
They call, Thistledown.

NORTHERN LIGHTS

Last night the light was burning and bright
O'er the cold clear Newfoundland sky,
And I wondered as I walked along the road,
If other men knew as I,
Such surging joy as overflowed
In breathless, pained delight,
The moment those brilliant northern beams
Flashed their patterns full on my sight.
And I thought as I made my way toward home,
To the music of splintering ice,
That to once view the dance
Of their flickering forms,
Would never, no never, suffice!

WIND SONG

Sing me the song of cattails and kelp,
Bachelor buttons and buttercups bent,
By the wild western will
Of the New World's wind,
Of thistles and clover, and alders that grow,
Where the shores are fast rockbound,
And New World winds blow.
Then sing me the song again and again,
That I of its sweet strains
Some note might sustain,
And blend my voice,
Like those gone before,
With the wild western will
Of the New World's wind.

SPARNIE TICKLES

Verse 1
When I was young, yes, just a boy,
I played beneath a friendly sky,
I swam in rivers full of joy,
With sparnie tickles swimming by.

Chorus:
Sparnie tickles in the stream,
Tiny fish that flash and gleam!
Sparnie tickles in the stream,
Swimming through my boyhood dream!

Verse 2
I played with friends long lost to me,
On a rocky island in the sea
We'd chase the girls, who'd laugh and scream
Then fish for sparnies in a stream.

Chorus
Sparnie tickles in the stream,
Tiny fish that flash and gleam!
Sparnie tickles in the stream,
Swimming through my boyhood dream!

Verse 3

The years have changed both you and me,
And those days can no longer be
The brook may still with sparnies teem.
But for us, now, they're just a dream.

Chorus

Sparnie tickles in the stream,
Tiny fish that flash and gleam!
Sparnie tickles in the stream,
Swimming through my boyhood dream!

Verse 4

Though life has led me far from home,
On the island where I used to roam,
In dreams I stroll through meadowland,
And fish the brooks of Newfoundland.

Chorus

Sparnie tickles in the stream,
Tiny fish that flash and gleam!
Sparnie tickles in the stream,
Swimming through my boyhood dream!

MY NEWFOUNDLAND

There is an island in the sea,
That calls in sacred tones to me,
A haven of rock and coarse gray sand,
My island home, my Newfoundland.

Sweep on ye ocean waves so brave,
O'er deep sea mountains, valleys, and caves,
Crash upon crag, rock-shore, and sand.
To rest on this island, this Newfoundland.

Mine are these hills with pine trees clad,
Land of the green, red and golden plaid.
Cloaked in white at winter's command,
Mine is this rock, called Newfoundland.

Oh, sing your stirring anthem song,
Tell of your mighty empire, strong,
But give me that rock with its coarse gray sand,
Give me my home, my Newfoundland!

Where men sing with silvern voices, clear,
Where storm gusts fret and eagles hear,
On mountain and moor I will take my stand,
For love of this place, my Newfoundland!

HERE

Here the morning tides
Tantalize the beach,
And gently run soft fingers
Through strands of silver hair.

Here the wild hawk hovers
In prelude to her plunge,
While piercing orbs in mid-air
Choose their breakfast fare.

Here majestic whales
Surface to gasp for breath,
Then slip beneath gray waters
To tangle in a net.

Here the northern storm gusts
Have beaten cliff rocks bare,
Till every mile of shoreline
Gives back a barren stare.

Here for countless generations
Of a gentle, peaceful race,
Have Indigenous people lived
In harmony with this place.

Here the flags of Europe
Have flown in centuries past,
In every cove and inlet,

From square sailed clipper masts
Here the smiles of lovers,
And children's laughter clear,
Have mingled with the voices,
Of a thousand summers fair.

And here the tears of widows,
Whose men were lost at sea,
Have splashed into the surf,
To be lost eternally.

THE VILLAGE AT DAWN

The frost-nipped snow creaks underfoot,
While the rooks fly aloft like windblown soot,
The pungent fragrance everywhere,
Of friendly woodsmoke in the air,
As drawn toward the early skies,
Sea mists, like ghosts, from their graves arise.
A field mouse darts beneath a mound,
Day's gentle stirrings all around,
As the little village nestled lays
'Twixt hills of olive pine tree sways.

THE AWAKENING

The timeless ties of family
Beckon us back today,
To the shores that bred our fathers,
Lands distant, far away,
Till in a seeming stranger,
With name akin to ours,
We find a long lost cousin,
Whose heritage we share.

And somewhere deep within us,
A slumbering chord is stirred,
To remind us of the union,
As blood returns to blood

NEWFOUNDLAND

The island of Newfoundland
Is mysterious and fair,
Where evergreen forests stalwart stand
And the Northern Lights flicker and flare.
Under its tuckamore, ptarmigan run
As joyful otters revel in river play,
Rompsing about in the summer sun,
While ruby-eyed loons call by night and day.
Here many a traveller has lost their way
When phantom bog lights have led them astray
And magical fairies with wings so bright'
'Tis said, fly freely in the moonlit night.
Rainbow trout, jumping, seem to dare
The hawks and eagles that hover and stare,
The spring-fed rivers and brooks run pure,
And tales of pirate treasure endure.
The roving moose and the roaming bear

Feast on the fruit of the chuckly pear,
While rabbits run through tamarack trails,
And kittiwakes call to humpback whales.

IRISH LULLABY

Sing me an old Irish lullaby.
Sing from your heart with a smile and sigh.
Sing with a voice all soothing and mild,
Like voices I heard when I was a child.
Sing while we watch the black birds flying high,
As we lie in the clover out under the sky!

OUT AROUND THE BAY

It's Christmas, and I fancy I can hear
The sound of the old-time sledge
Out around the bay.
I hear the driver coaxing the mare
As they glide through Backhouse Cove,
Along the silent bay.
Maybe a Roberts or an Anstey boy,
With a load of wood and Christmas cheer
For someone in the bay.

No doubt, there will be some mummers along,
And cake and syrup or something strong
To warm them on their way.
You can count on music, laughter and love,
For 'tis Christmas in the outport coves,
Out around the bay!

FLYING SAUCER

I remember one Christmas when I was a boy.
How I longed to have a particular toy,
An aluminum disk about three feet wide,
On which I could sit for a downhill ride.
It had woven handles, one on each side,

And, oh! How that polished saucer could slide!
Designed for one, it could hold three or four,
But as we were kids, we piled on some more.
From the top of the highest snow hill in town,
We all jumped aboard and started down!

Now, sleds and toboggans are all very good,
But polished aluminum goes faster than wood.
About halfway down was a rounded lump,
That was simply referred to as,
"The Bump"!

How fast we were going, God only knows,
A bundle of bodies in thick winter clothes.
Partway down we had lost at least two
But what with the speed and the spinning, who knew?
Suddenly one terrorized soul cried, "The Bump!"
And we struck that obstacle with an almighty whump!
Charlene went one way, Derek went another!
I prayed a prayer for my sister and brother!

I held those red straps with a dead man's grip,
And flew on alone in my silver spaceship.
Eventually gravity slowed me down.
I felt like I'd slid to the edge of town!

When the world stopped spinning, I got to my feet,
And started back up to see who I'd meet.
Charlene was OK but all in a crump,
Then Derek came by rubbing his rump.
Our uphill struggle was long and slow,
Then we climbed back on for another go!

This poem is for the poet's siblings, Charlene R. (Harbin) Van Maren
and Derek Laite Harbin. Those were the days.

A LITTLE BAG OF CLAY

I have a small brown bag of clay
From our back yard where I used to play,
I gathered it with a childish hand,
Just a little bag of dry rock sand.
We sold the house and moved away,
So very many years ago;
Yet, I still can't bring myself
To let that symbol go.
It holds a wealth of sunny hours,
A small boy's rhapsodies,
And I guess I'll always treasure it;
A little bag of clay.

THANK YOU, GOD, FOR MY GRAY CAT

Thank-you, God, for my gray cat,
Even though she's very fat.
Mommy says that any day,
Baby cats may come to stay.

Daddy says they may not stay.
He says some may go away.
Baby brother will keep one,
If it's cute and lots of fun.

But whatever happens then,
Will my cat get thin again?
My friend, Sarah, says 'tis so.
Sarah's six, and ought to know!

AND EVEN NOW

Church bells early in the morn,
Or late as evening shades are drawn
Cause my heart to wend its way,
Back memory's old familiar path,
To Sunday School, and home, and you.
Do you perhaps remember, still,
The games we used to play,
The cardboard forts we carved and manned
With plastic cowboy toys?

Our toboggan runs on snow hills high,
And the floor that served as a skating rink?
Our boxing matches in the basement,
Our bedroom catapults?
Yes, those were carefree days and fun,
And even now, they bring a smile.

But the years have laid those times to rest
In memory's thickly padded nest.
Now our days are different to be sure,
For now we know that life holds more
Than the childish games we knew back then.

Life is hard and cold at times,
And its courses, hard to run.
Yet even in the darkest hours,

When homely joys seem far removed,
It's good to know there is a Friend,
Whose loving arms once held us close,
And even so may do again.

'Tis a well-remembered thought, as well,
That though our paths may separate,
The music of an old church bell,
Can join our hearts 'round memory's gate.

THE ROCKING HORSE

The old metal rocking horse we rode,
Has carried its final childish load.
It sat on Grandma's porch for years,
Transporting us all to wild frontiers.

Its spotted flanks and deep brown eyes
Would forward bend, and dip and rise.
So long it guarded the big house well,
Till they carted it out to the shady dell
Where it spent its twilight years alone,
And rust o'ertook the spotted roan.

It was thought of lightly then, I know,
As we clambered on to have a go;
Now the metal's rusted, the stirrup's slack,
But oh! Earth's millions to have it back!

PANCAKE DAY

Hooray! Hooray! It's Pancake Day!
The day to put the yeast away.
Mother is in the kitchen now.

Look at the pancake stacks! Oh! Wow!
Most will have fortune signs within,
Some, no doubt plain, with nothing in.
Use your fork to prod and poke,
Or you might accidentally choke!

A shopkeeper's sign is a piece of string,
You'll be first to marry if you find a ring!
A button's a sign of a tailor to be,
A toothpick or nail means carpentry.
A straw means you'll be a poor housewife,
But a coin means you'll have a wealthy life*!*

NEWFOUNDLAND OUTINGS

I remember picnic lunches
In rock-infested fields,
And boiled up Jiggs dinners
On shores of ocean stone,
Lobsters flicking frantically,
Striking terror in the hearts
Of youngsters in a sixties station wagon.
And then, the long drive home,
And bedtime under a mountain of quilts.
And, oh, to be a boy again,
In rural Newfoundland!

WINGS

Oh for wings I knew as a boy!
Wings of freedom! Wings of joy!
Wings of endless happy days,
Spent in Terra Nova bays.
Not real wings but wings I felt,
Watching snowfields warm and melt,
Wings that lifted me as I ran,
Wings oft' folded in the man.
Oh for my childhood's laughing joy!
Oh for wings!
To be a boy!

FOR NORMA AT THIRTEEN

Child of the windswept ocean town,
Where the fog drifts in and settles down
Upon steep hills of evergreen,
There are many places you've never been,
So much of life you have not seen.
Wish not the years of youth away;
Life's sights and sounds will have their day.
The time may come, when with hopes cast down,
You yearn for your misty ocean town,
And the tones of childhood's carefree song,
And the youthful years that seemed so long.

*Norma H. Decker of Ming's Bight, Newfoundland, the
talent behind ND Photography, is the subject of this poem.*

LOVE'S HAUNT

When music pure like sainthood's breath,
Sweeps o'er the harp strings of my heart,
And voices smooth as milky babes
Caress my ears in velvet warmth,
My mind does conjure up your image then,
And love's sweet death is born in me again.

And how can I be spared such poignancy,
When every scented blossom speaks of thee?

Oh, stay the spell and set me free,
Or in full union let us be,
Till life itself forgets its birthing ways,
And Father Time forgoes to count his days.

HOW MANY CUPS

How many cups of tea did we drink
As we sat 'round the table across from the sink?
And how many cookies did Grandfather swipe
Behind Grandma's back as he gave us a wink?

How many cups did we drink by the shore?
Must have been hundreds, maybe more,
Gazing out at the rocks and waves,
As we sat on the bridge by the old back door.

How many times was it just you and me,
As we chatted about friends and family?
How many cups of tea did we drink,
Just by ourselves, or with company?
How many times was the kettle put on,
Late at night or at the crack of dawn?

Yes, and how often as we drank our tea
Did we have a wee snack, a bun or a scone?
How many heartaches and how many woes
Did the cups of tea soothe? A few I suppose.
But the love and comfort that came with the tea?
A million or more! God only knows.

TEA

Verse 1

In Newfoundland outports around the bay,
Tea was everywhere back in the day.
'Twas thought of as a national drink,
Served with a lunch, a yarn and a wink!

Chorus

Steep the leaves till the tea is black,
Stir it clockwise, but never turn back!
Stir the pot once, but never more,
And tell me stories from day of yore.

Verse 2

A head count was the tea's measurement,
As into the silver pot it went,
A spoonful for each, and one for the pot,
Then scald the cups to make them hot.

Chorus

Steep the leaves till the tea is black,
Stir it clockwise, but never turn back!
Stir the pot once, but never more,
And tell me stories from days of yore.

Verse 3

Tune the radio to Gerald S. Doyle,
Hear news while you let the water boil,
When the kettle steam is three feet high,
You'll brew the tea, and cut the pie.

Chorus

Steep the leaves till the tea is black,
Stir it clockwise, but never turn back!
Stir the pot once, but never more,
And tell me stories from days of yore.

Verse 4

Yes, tea was the order of the day,
In each fishing village in every bay.
The tales they'd spin were sometimes tall,
And the yarns weren't always in a ball

Chorus

Steep the leaves till the tea is black,
Stir it clockwise, but never turn back!
Stir the pot once, but never more,
And tell me stories from days of yore.

OUTPORT KITCHEN

Pot steam,
And wood heat,
Fisherman's brewis for dinner,
Blueberry duff dessert,
Prepared by hands so experienced
They can do it without a thought.

The knitting bag overflows
With sweaters and spreads
In the making,
Worsted socks hanging to dry,
Over the stove,
Plastic plants on doilies,
To brighten up the room,
And the unmistakable smell,
Of balsam from the yard.

MAYMIE

Your graceful hospitality,
Your cheerful words and smile,
Make each hour spent in your company
A memory well worthwhile.
Your treasured tours of Twillingate
With historic culture filled,
Are rich in wisdom's golden weight,
Grains of knowledge finely milled.
Beyond mere grace and history,
Remembered smiles at tea,
A stronger tie fast binds our hearts -
One blood, one family.

Harbin and cousin, Mary ("Maymie") Roberts-Hewlett,) were close friends, and in her later years they spent many happy hours together in Twillingate. He enjoyed her wise and witty company! She was the first cousin of his grandfather, Andrew Harbin.

RAINBOW ON A PLATE

The Newfoundland cold plate
Is a visual treat!
Yellow mustard salad,
Creamy coleslaw so sweet!
Jellies of red, yellow, orange or green
Potatoes stained purple with pickled beet.
Bright red tomatoes on lettuce so lean
Beside varied hues of thinly sliced meat.
A splotch of cranberry sauce, so bright
Partridge berries in a raspberry gel,
A little savory stuffing as well.
Potatoes speckled with carrots and peas,
There's a rainbow of delight
On my plate, if you please!

WEREN'T WE RICH!

Oh, for wet beach rocks and ocean swells!
The sweetly pungent woodland smells!
Blustering winds, we wrestled against,
Never a worry, nor thought of angst.
Running up hills through morning dews,
Indulging in free oceanic views.
Weren't we rich! How could we be poor!

Chasing our friends across the grouse moor.
Ah, for the simple times we shared,
Red and white punts in the salt sea breeze,
Heedless of rabbits and wrens that stared
From lupine-lined shores with twisted trees,

Hot bread and jam, the crock of sweet beans,
Jiggs dinner with pudding, fresh turnip greens!
The pot-belly stove, wood piled by the door,
Weren't we rich! How could we be poor!

LOUIS DYER'S CAMP

Louis Dyer built a camp.
Inside it was a trifle damp.
In spite of all the scorners' wit,
Louis built and wouldn't quit.

The camp was only four' by six'
And built of wooden stakes and sticks,
But, inside, Louis found a place,
Untouched by life's frustrating pace.

And so, though some may stop and jeer
At that humble camp not far from here,
They never dream that Lou has found,
A place where joy and peace abound

When Harbin taught at Ming's Bight in October, 1979, Louis Dyer was one of his students.

STEW REGULAR'S SKI-DOO

Stew Regular was a brave soul,
A mighty man was he,
He bought himself a new Ski-doo
When he was eighty-three.

His poor wife's heart did flutter,
To see him drive so fast.
She said, "He is fair silly.
He'll kill himself at last!"

He rode past woodland valley,
O'er peaks both high and low,
The rough trail not created
Through which he dared not go.

Till one day in a fine blizzard,
Fit to frighten you out of your gizzard,
He spilled upon a juniper stump
That left him with a wonderful lump.

Said Stew to his worried wife, Sarah,
"'Twas the stumps I should have been 'ware a!
Now my money is gone, my Ski-doo well broke,
And the lump on my head is so sore!
I wish I had listened at once when you spoke,
And stayed healthy, as I was before!"

The truth may be slightly exaggerated in this tall tale. Stewart and Sarah Regular of Ming's Bight became dear friends when Harbin taught in Ming's ight. Harbin dedicates this poem to them and the memories of their gracious hospitality and company.

I WONDER WHY?

And I remember when Gordon Clarke's
House burned down at Ming's Bight.
Something about the furnace they said,
It's hard to remember now.

The car keys were in the house,
So we carried the car across the road
To his son's driveway, the camper, too.
We threw water on the houses nearby
To keep them from catching as well.
There was no fire pump in the town,
So we formed a bucket brigade
Down to the beach,

But it was no use,
The house was gone by then.
We could only stand and watch,

As everything they'd ever owned
Went up in smoke and soot.
When, finally, the walls fell in,

We all began to leave.
On the way home,
We met the fire truck from Baie Verte,
The Mountie got there first.
Everyone nodded and said,
"What a shame,"

Then turned again toward home,
To see what we could collect and give
To get them on their feet again.

I guess we all did what we could,
But I know it wasn't enough.
They're building a new house now
In the very same spot,
And the town still has
No fire equipment.
I wonder why?

Something about government funds

THE STIRLING NIGHTINGALE

Hark! The Stirling Nightingale
Performs a song for angel ears!
Her lyric voice bespeaks
A heart beyond her years.
She lifts glad notes of human pen
To heaven's portalled walls,
Then alluringly withdraws again
Her mystic treble calls
To shower them upon men's heads,
In gilded music halls.

Georgina Stirling of Twillingate, Newfoundland became a world class opera star, known as the "Nightingale of the North", in the 1890's. She died in 1935. This poem is a tribute to her, a family friend of the Harbins.

SHADOWS

In old Newfoundland the ancient hills
Reached for each other across steep fjords,
And silvery water flowed in rills
Past battlefields where English Lords
With France's armies crossed their swords.
Great river waves and tumbling falls
Echoed their music off mamateek walls,
Where red ochre painted families slept
While diving loons voiced their haunting calls,
And caribou danced, and willows wept.
In spring Arctic ice floes drifted past
Carrying white-coated seals at play,
As floating mountains of aqua ice
Their stretching sunset shadows cast.
And still, today, those timeworn hills
Reach for each other athwart steep fjords,
Where silver water flows in rills.
And, yet, are the sunset shadows deep,
The diving loons makes their haunting calls,
And caribou dance as willows weep.

THE LEAK

The leak in my room, so sullen, bare,
Arrests my early morning stare.
It's mildewed rim, creeping, brown,
Aspires to bring the whole roof down.
And what the lesson taught today
By this somewhat decadent display?
A fact too often got around,
Man's works, like men, die and decay.

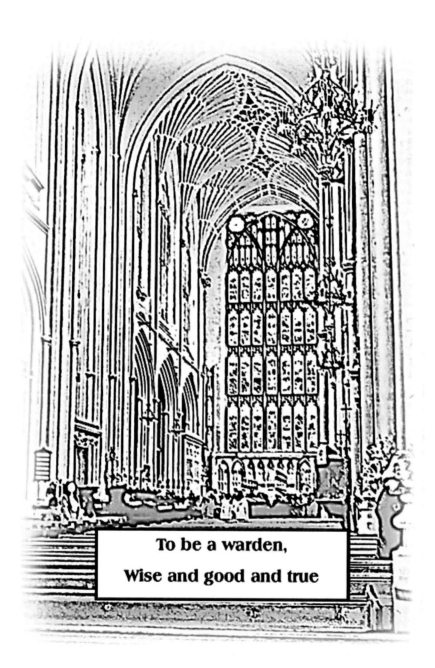

To be a warden,
Wise and good and true

PARISH REGISTERS

Page after faded page,
Of names, dates and towns,
The last remaining record
Of brawny sea-tanned men,
And strong-willed women,
Whose lust for life and adventure
Drove them to the rock-bound coasts,
Of an island in a brooding sea.
The dust of generations
Preserved within each cover,
Is all that's left to tell
Of their hopes, their joys and sorrows,
Whose descended heirs we are,
Who scan these lines today?

What of the dreams
That brought them here,
Or the fears for all we know,
And 'neath what banner stood they,
When facades were wiped away?

Did they find whate'er they sought
In coming to this place,
Those youths and maids of whom
These books are one last trace?
Do those self-same burning passions,

That swirled within their veins,
Still live themselves out fully
in the blood of you and me?
Page after faded page,
Of names, dates and towns,
Till my eyes begin to swim,

And my mind reels so with the weight of it,
That I return the book to its shelf,
And call it all a day.
But I'll return again tomorrow,
To browse and search some more,
In the faded Parish Registers,
'Til I find the long-lost forebears
I came here searching for.

NEVER

I never met John Cabot,
Still, I know he sailed this sea.
I have never flown like puffins fly,
Yet, I'm sure they feel quite free.
I have never heard an angel,
Yet I believe they live above.
I have never seen God's image,
Yet, I've learned to trust His love.

TWO ROCKS

Two Rocks have shaped my life,
And from their smitten forms,
I have drawn much strength and fortitude,
To weather many storms.

The first of these, my island home,
For which my forebears left
England's shores forever behind,
Nor thought themselves bereft.

The latter Rock much older is
Than the Newfoundland I love;
His Name, a force that draws mankind
To fairer worlds above.

Two Rocks have formed my present life,
Two Rocks that stalwart stand,
Yeone of them in peace reclines
Within the other's hand.

In this poem, Harbin honours his mother, Alma Blanche (Laite)
Harbin. It was written when she was hospitalized after hip
replacement surgery in the early 1980's.

THE WHITE WOODEN CHURCH

Love like a sea is surrounding me,
As I sit in the white wooden church,
Where the old rugged cross
That shall suffer no loss,
Is held high for all who search
For the lingering peace,
And the joyous release,
So well-known in the white wooden church;
As known as the rungs and rails of these chairs,
So intimately acquainted with prayers;
As known and as much a part of this place,
As the cross, and the tear-stained
Altar of Grace.

WITH WHAT GRACE

Lo, with what grace,
The Island greets its own;
It welcomes them with warm embrace,
Bone of its very bone!

GRACE SUFFICIENT

O Merciful Father in Heaven above,
Look down on Thy child in tender love,
And, by Thy compassionate, strong embrace,
Impart an added measure of grace,
Grace to forgive the hurts of the past,
Grace for today's woes, as long as they last,
Grace to forgive, to endure, to forget,
And grace to remember Thy goodness yet.

LORD, GIVE ME A SONG

Lord, give me a song through everything,
So shall I sing praises to my King!
Give me each day a gladsome smile,
To show forth Your presence all the while.
Lend me a tender word to speak,
That others may sense Your Spirit, meek.
Lord, grant that in all I say or do,
My heart and mind will stay true to You;
And ever let Your praises be rung,
Wherever the song of my heart is sung!

DEEP WATERS

Lord, speak to me now.
My heart is soft,
And pliable to your touch;
The truths you speak
Will find a mark,
Deep within my soul.
In lighter moments
When all seemed well,
My attentions wandered far.
I found no time
To ponder long,
The insights of Your Word.
But now, perhaps,
When joy seems muted,
And merrier times have flown,
With wisdom I
Shall begin to know,
Even as I am known.

A STEWARD

O God, let me live
To give to others
Out of the bounty
You have given me.
For all that I own
And all I call mine,
I count as a loan,
Really it is Thine.

And, oh, I do want
To be a warden,
Wise and good and true,
Of everything I have,
And everything I do,
That through all my days,
Poems, songs and gifts,
Your will might be done,
With gratitude and praise.,
With gratitude and praise

AS DAY BEGINS

Give pure peace; grant great grace,
And make us strong to run apace.
The waiting world a challenge holds,
As another day by faith unfolds.
Let not life's circumstantial test
Remove our hearts from out the rest
Gained leaning hard upon Thy breast

It was a day when
an island's youth
Might have courted
love
on a rocky beach

LAND CLAIMS

O rugged hills, O ragged trees,
Whose land is this,
Whose waters these,
That rise and fall
In heaving sighs,
Beneath the island's
Proud pale skies?

Tell me, if at all you can,
Whence travelled these rivers
Since they first ran?
Whose streams are these,
And whose the rocks,
That form their flashing
Silvern locks?

Europeans came but late.
Indigenous Peoples'
Relics date.
Whose then the regal
Rock-horned hills,

Whose forms though dismal
Yield sweet rills?
O rugged hills, O ragged trees,

God's land is this!
God's waters these,
That rise and fall
In heaving sighs,
Beneath the Island's
Proud pale skies.

NEWFOUNDLAND'S REVIVAL SONG

"Times, they were hard here once, my son.
All we had then was fish and pork fat,
A kettle of tea, and a homemade bun.
But along came Joey, who changed all that.
He brought us wealth and pride again,
In giving us Confederation.
Some called it foolish, and said 'twas in vain.
Now we know different; we've proved this nation."

That's what they told me in childhood,
Old folks answering a child's demand.
It was the story of Joey Smallwood,
And such was the song of Old Newfoundland..

SHIPS IN FOG

I see the ships pass by,
Not knowing what their cargoes are,
Nor where their home ports lie,
And ever as I watch them from
My window on the shore,
I imagine they are pirate ships
From out the Island's yore.

I dream John Pike has captured them,
From an English merchant fleet
Returning from some far-off place,
Where the air is warm and sweet.

I fancy there is gold on board,
From another pirate's hoard,
Or maybe robes and jeweled rings,
Once worn by wealthy kings.

And as the ships drift out of sight
Into the dense sea fog,
I interrupt my dream to feed
The stove another log.

THE FLAG OF NEWFOUNDLAND

The flag! The flag! Our noble flag!
Our provincial banner true.
Sing loud the worthy praises of
The yellow, red and blue!

Give honour, laud and loyalty
The stately flag unto,
And let its colours warm our hearts,
The yellow, red and blue!

The flag! The flag! Our own fair flag!
Though its pattern yet be new,
Has now our high allegiance won,
The yellow, red and blue!

CRIMSON STAINED THE BLUE PUTTEES

It was a summer day in rural France,
The first of thirty-one that month,
A day refreshed by a warm soft breeze,
When crimson stained the blue puttees.

It was a day when an island's youth
Might have courted love on a rocky beach,
Or 'neath the birch and maple trees,
The day crimson stained the blue puttees.
'Twas a day of uniforms and guns,
And barbed wire stretched across the land,
When dashing boys fell to their knees,
As crimson stained the blue puttees.

It was summertime in rural France,
When bullets rained through skeleton trees
On lads from Twillingate and Harbour Main,
And crimson stained the blue puttees.

Lance Corporal Wilfred Thomas Harbin of willingate, the younger brother of Harbin's grandfather, was killed in action at the age of nineteen, July 1, 1916 in the Battle of Beaumont Hamel, France. This poem is dedicated to the memory of Newfoundland's first 500 soldiers, and all subsequent young men who volunteered for active service in World War I.

ON REFLOATING THE WILLIAM CARSON

Four hundred feet deep the Carson lies,
In the North Atlantic Sea.
Now there's talk of bringing her up again,
To salvage and retrieve.
No doubt some goods may be regained,
Some treasured belongings found,
But I'm afraid the cookies
In my grandfather's car,
Will do just as well unfound.

The M. V. William Carson sank in June 1977 while travelling between Lewisporte, Newfoundland and the coast of Labrador. Harbin's Grandmother Laite's car was on board being shipped to her grandson, Derek Harbin, in Labrador. She had baked cookies and laid them on the back seat for him as a surprise.

COD MORATORIUM

He sits on the stage, looking out to sea,
His ankles feel fettered although he is free.
His boat, tethered tight to the tilting pier,
Shudders in mute, unaccustomed fear.

His story is simple, his pleasures are few,
His history old, his circumstance new.
His black sou'wester's on a rusty nail,
And the fishing shack is but a jail.

His father's, father's, father's sire,
Fished these waters with one desire,
To take from the bounty of the sea,
Enough to feed his family.

And those who lived and died between,
Lived each the same, and died serene,
Nor dreamed of wealth and castles high,
Nor doubted God, nor asked Him, "Why?"

They lived and loved and called this home,
This land of rock, this isle of stone,
Learned lessons of wisdom from the sea,
Of perseverance in adversity.
Their wills became stout, their muscles strong,
Their laughter plenty, their patience long.
They learned to depend on none but themselves,

And told mystic stories of lights and elves.
And long their distinctive culture grew,
Unknown to many, admired by few,
Save those who came occasionally
To laugh at them, to pillage the sea.

Fool hearts! They tried in their small boats
To compete with giant trawler throats,
Strove to preserve their simple ways,
As had their fathers in bygone days.

But the tiny boats their match had met.
Lines can't compete with miles of net,
And the foreign ships took all they would,
Till the sea had given all she could.

Now the bureaucrats in their towers, high,
Are concerned that all the fish may die,
So they've taken his right to fish away,

To return it or not, they'll decide, someday.
The foreign trawlers still ply their trade,
Beyond our borders, just a shade,
While the fisherman, sitting on the stage,
Looks out to sea and swallows his rage.

Give him a handout from pity or guilt,
Think not of his life on the fishery built.
Turn away from his questioning honesty,
And clear-eyed, silent dignity.

RESETTLEMENT

Whose home this was I cannot tell,
This broken, empty, old gray shell.
Its mildewed walls are stained and brown,
The ceilings throughout are sagging down.
Each floor is piled high with junk,
Photographs, clothes, a rusted trunk.
The wall hangings here are all askew,
Antiques and mementoes left behind,
Discarded in favour of something new,
Because someone said they would find,
Life much easier and really grand,
In a bigger settlement on the mainland.

HOUSE BY THE STAGE

The house by the tilting, time-worn stage
Is a remnant of another age,
Clinging precariously to the cliff,
Like a gull on the bow of a fishing skiff.
Its unhinged doors sag and creak,
And its shingled roof knows many a leak.
The wind-rustled rags of curtains hang
In shuttered windows that squeak and bang,
The fine English china long used for tea,
Lies in scattered, fragmented gentility.
And the passing tourist that happens by,
Can but dream of the stories that forever lie
Sealed in the dusty muted walls,
Of the house by the stage as it leans and falls.

THE VILLAGE THAT WAS

Hang ye down, ye ferns of the island's green wood,
Hang ye low with bowed heads, as ever ye should.
Weep tears from each frond as ye stand in the rain,
Let the wind through the willows echo your pain.
No more do light footfalls of the children of men
Sound through the tuckamore atop your wild fen,
For gone is the village that stood on your shore,
And the lights of its dwellings shine out no more.

Now few men there remain who ever have seen
Life in these abandoned houses that lean
Precariously close to the deep green sea,
That patiently waits to hide them from me,
Till time has erased, as time always does,
last vestiges of the village that was.

O NEWFOUNDLAND, BRAVE NEWFOUNDLAND

O Newfoundland, Brave Newfoundland!
Fair Island of the Sea,
Upon whose far-north, rock-bound shores
I would much sooner be!

O Newfoundland, Brave Newfoundland!
Protect those dearest me,
And in your kind arms cradle them
Till I return to thee!

O Newfoundland, Brave Newfoundland!
However long life's race,
Within the cloister of my heart,
None else shall take thy place.

ON CREATING A MYTHOLOGY
FOR
THE LAND OF TERRA NOVA

Vaughn Harbin is inventing his own mythology for Newfoundland, a tradition of folklore that teaches the values of a place through the use of legend, fable, saga or allegory. The Kalen of Klyn poems and Aurina are examples of this ongoing project

Aurina is the Queen of the midnight winds of spring that gently warm the island.

Knights of Terra Nova (Newfoundland) never roamed the barrens of the Avalon. Harbin imagines what their characters and quests might have been had they existed

Where, once,

there stood the Kingdom of Klyn,

In every world, a world within

AURINA

Aurina,
Silver-haired queen of the midnight wind
From off the North Atlantic's waves,
That break and roll on the rockbound coasts
Of Terra Nova's ancient form,
Bring new and sweet-spiced, southern scents,
And gently warm the Island's caves,
stunted spruce, and scattered stones.
Bind in Purgatorian chains
The slivery, icy-tongued blasts
Of Demeter's saddened state.

THE KINGDOM OF KLYN

Where now the oceanic Barrens lie,
Beneath fair Newfoundland's azure sky,
There once stood the mystic Kingdom of Klyn,
In every world, a world within.

And even now there are those who say,
If you stand in the still of an autumn day,
As the Avalon mists go drifting by,
You may hear in the wind a haunting sigh,
In Elysian tones, ethereal, high.
It drifts from heights where white seabirds fly,
Through moorland mists that are wafted by
To where willow ptarmigan nod their heads
As they nest in mossy heather beds,
And where the spruce grouse run through tuckamore
On bluffs above the Atlantic's shore.
For, those who love this land today,

Be they young and strong, or stooped and gray,
Regardless of the race they claim,
Or religion, wealth, rank or name,
Oft' bear in aspect, tongue, or grace,
Of Klyn's lost Kingdom, the final trace.

And when they lift silvern voices high
To tune these rills, Klyn doth reply!
Then saffron bakeapples ripen to gold,
And partridgeberries sweeten with cold,

Just as they did eons ago
When singers of Klyn sang "io! io!"
Celebrating the greatness of God,
Whom they knew by the blessings of the sod,
And creatures that swim, and creep, and fly,
And wonders of ocean, earth and sky.
Though they knew not His Name as we today,
They worshiped Him in their own way,

Lauding Him for His goodness to them
With gifts of bright gold and blue-green gem.
Their peaceful Kingdom enjoyed many years
Prosperously, without foes or fears,
Till there came a time when evil grew strong,
And sought to do the Kingdom wrong,

So Klyn's knights learned skills of battle and war,
Defeating armies, wizards and more.
Then the realms of men and elves sought peace,
And worked together to great increase,
Till both their domains waxed rich and good,
As men ruled the moors and elves the wood.

They called those times their Golden Age,
Writing their tales on the parchment page.
Men built homes of stone on the Barrens' hills,
And drank sweet water from flowing rills
That emptied themselves into the bays
To the North and South of the moorland haze.

Elves made their dwellings in woodland trees
Near shady bowers and lowland lees,
Drinking sweet nectar of Labrador teas,
Eating the honey of golden bees.

New eras came and ages went,
As aspens trembled and balsams bent,
Before the Elves, and men of Klyn
Faced anew the threat of evil within.

But the Wanton came and reared its head
When the Prince of Klyn fair Aleah wed,
And though that demon met his demise,
Never again did the Kingdom rise
To the glories it had known before,
As it stood on proud Terra Nova's shore

Though Aleah's crystal vial she wore
Saved Khalen and brought him to health once more,
When wounded, he lay on the battlefield,
Bereft of arrow, and sword, and shield.

Klyn, itself, lay in ruin that day,
And all that remains of it to this day
Are the rocks that on the Barrens lie
Beneath fair Terra Nova's sky,
Where once there stood the Kingdom of Klyn,
In every world, a world within.

Though all those figures are long since gone,
Beauteous voices yet call from the sea.
Fair Aleah! Brave Khalen! They call to me!

And over the mist-shrouded mournful moor,
I hear the wind wailing evermore,
For that world in every world within;
For Aleah and Khalen pleading for Klyn,
And a wondrous world that once had been,
The world that was the Kingdom of Klyn.

Written on August 25, 2020 at the request of his friend, Jaspreet Singh Dhala, the magic of this poem emerged. In Harbin's words, "Jaspreet Singh Dhala's help in preparing this poetry manuscript for publication has been invaluable.

THE KNIGHTS OF TERRA NOVA

Not since ancient Tara stood,
In field of stone near standing wood,
Not since Glastonbury's walls,
Stood strong beside Arthurian halls,
Nor yet since knights of the crusades
Breached Middle Eastern palisades,
Have hearts as true, have souls as bright
As those of Terra Nova knights,
Graced terrestrial forests fair,
And breathed pure sainthood's virgin air.

And what though they be rare, be few?
What if their steps but press the dew,
Then disappear in misted sun,
Where silver fox and ermine run?
Love is their prod, Truth be their quest!
Their hearts are free, and triple blest,
Integrity of soul, of mind,
And certainty that they shall find,
Somewhere upon their island sod,
A path that leads to Truth and God.

ALEAH OF KLYN

In ancient days in Newfoundland,
Long ere the Norseman saw the sand
And rocks of Terra Nova's shores,
And ages before European wars,
There stood the ancient Kingdom of Klyn,
In every world, a world within.
Of all brave youths and maidens fair
Who lived and breathed the Island's air,
The purest of soul and fairest of face,
Who ever the Kingdom of Klyn did grace,
Was Aleah of Klyn, the Northern Rose,
Who dwelt where the laurel and rosemary grew,
And whose clear and beauteous voice was heard
As she sang by the bay to the white seabird,
Whose cries as he hovered overhead,
Told her the mysteries of the world, 'tis said.

She was born of both human and elven kin,
And carried the best of both within,
And Aleah grew wise, and good and fair,
With emerald eyes and auburn hair,
And was loved by the King of Klyn's own son,
Prince Khalen, of knight's, the bravest one!

The Prince and Aleah were wed in June,
'Neath the silver orb of a gibbous moon,
And seabirds sang in the starry sky,

Where now the wasted barrens lie,
And where once there stood the Kingdom of Klyn,
In every world, a world within.

The late Brenda Workman, of Montreal, Quebec, Vaughn's close friend and teaching colleague, first suggested that Harbin should write this poem. He says. "Thank you, Brenda, for loving my poetry as you did!"

KHALEN OF KLYN

Where now the wasted Barrens lie
Beneath fair Terra Nova's sky,
Here, once, there stood the Kingdom of Klyn,
In every world a world within.

All was quiet in the evening air,
And the silence seemed tangible everywhere,
When out of the darkening forest glade
Rode the Horseman of Klyn with his fearsome blade
Held high in a hand adrip with blood,
Came Khalen of Klyn with thundering thud
Of iron-hooved horse a spattering the mud,
Came Khalen of Klyn adrip with blood!

The silver orbed moon shone in dim disarray
As the vanishing horseman sped away.
Over the foothills, across the plain,
To the outskirts of the Elven domain,
Then on through the shimmering silver shade,
On to the Elven King's stockade!

Like the cresting wave of river in flood,
Came Khalen of Klyn adrip with blood!
The heart of the Elven King turned cold
At the sound of the message Prince Khalen told,
When with sword held high and thundering thud,
Came Khalen of Klyn adrip with blood.

Quoth the King in royal anger rude,
"It is enough! This viper's brood
That stalks the Elven forest's shade,
Shall lately taste keen Elven blade!

But softly now, my Princely One!
What hast the Wasting Wanton done?
How now thy royal figure slips;

The rosy colour flees thy lips!
To the Prince, fair courtiers one and all!
There spread thine arms to break his fall.
Thus steady his arm, his foot, his hip.
Khalen of Klyn is with blood adrip!"

"Nay! Nay! O King of the Magic Wood!
My wounds but bleed as pure hearts should,
Whene'er is heard the Wanton's wail
Within the green and peaceful vale.
Grieve not for princely knighthood's pain,

For, wounds as these, I count as gain.
Each suffered not its pulsing flow
Until it, too, had dealt a blow."
And so, they helped him to his steed.
And so, he led them with all speed,
Till they came within the Wanton's rage,
Prince and pauper and King and page.

For the Wasting Wanton, the Devil's churl,
Sought the soul of every boy and girl,
And had vowed to keep them forever bound
In a place ever lost, in a land never found!

They fought him brave! They fought him strong!
They battled the Wasting Wanton long,
Till there stood but a man 'twixt Heav'n and Hell,
And, then, the valiant Khalen fell!

But not before his princely blade
A fearsome mortal wound had made,
Deep in the heart of the Wanton's breast.

Fair Khalen of Klyn, forever blest!
Scarce yet a day had passed its shade
Since the horseman of Klyn with his fearsome blade,
Held high in a hand adrip with blood,
Had ridden the forest spattering the mud.

But, oh, for the Kingdom of King bereft!
Oh, for the pitiful remnant left.

And, ah, for the women of Klyn who sought
Their sons alive and found them not.
Like sparrows and wrens in the evening sky,
That to their nestlngs homeward fly,
So had their gallant spirits flown,
By pure angelic zephyrs blown.

Upon the moor a lone heart kneels,
Mid heaven's spark and thunder peals.
'Tis Aleah of Klyn, the Northern Rose,

Upon whose face the North wind blows!
Could writer tell!,
Could artist show,
Such drama framed against the glow
Of muted mauve voluminous cloud,
As fair Aleah's figure, bowed!

Her noble face o'er Khalen's, pale.
Her billowing cape in the gathering gale!
Her words of Love, his fading breath;
Lips red with life, lips pale with death!
With the auburn silk of her tresses fair,

With feminine glory, with her own hair
She wiped the tears of pain that told
Alone, how suffered the knight so bold.
And as his eyelids struggled to ope',
Her heart beat rose in rhythmic hope,

And willed warm life into his form,
Her breast a fury, her love a storm!
"Foul Hell beneath! Fair Heaven above!
Touch not the soul of the man I love!"
She cried, with hands stretched in the air,
Wild flames of passion in her auburn hair!

All is silent, now, in the breaking dawn,
And all these figures, long since gone.
Where, now, the wasted Barrens lie
Beneath fair Terra Nova's sky,
A beauteous voice calls from the sea.
Fair Aleah? Brave Khalen? Who calls to me?
Here, once, there stood the Kingdom of Klyn.
In every world a world within!

And over the mist-shrouded, mournful moor,
Is heard the wind wailing evermore,
For a world in every world within,
And Aleah, pleading, for Khalen of Klyn.
'Tis Aleah, pleading, for Khalen of Klyn!
Aleah is pleading…for Khalen of Klyn!

THE WASTING WANTON OF KLYN

Since ever the Kingdom of Klyn began,
In a time long lost to elves and man,
Forces of evil, malice and sin,
Threatened and warred, and strove to win
Victory over the Kingdom of Klyn,
In every world, a world within.
The most fiendish and loathsome of them all
To cast o'er the Kingdom a darksome pall,
Was the Wasting Wanton, all that remained
Of a bitter life by hate sustained.

Soram the Sullen, as he was first called
Lived in a fortress of granite, thick-walled.
His manner was ever evil and vile,
And his temper at best took little to rile.
Surrounded by shadowed dank that creeps,
And frost-shattered boulders in mountainous heaps,
He grew twisted by day and wicked by night,

Till none recognized him by name or sight.
Woe to the one whose heart departs,
To follow the ways of the devil's arts!
So Sorum the Sullen, the Wanton became,
And all who lived shuddered at the name,
Of him who dwelt in the murk and the dun,
And the umbra vales that knew no sun.

The Wanton had once been human, 'twas said,
And desired Aleah of Klyn to wed,
But she was betrothed to Khalen, a knight,
Who was heir to the Kingdom of Klyn so bright,
And whose father, King Lem, reigned from the throne
Of flashing blue-green and golden-red stone,
Which was known to all as the Stone of Light,
And which men today call, Labradorite.

Queen Palina the Wise, wife of King Lem,
Blessed the newlyweds and gave to them
Two wondrous gifts, a golden fife,
And a crystal vial of Elixir of Life,
From her Northland home where icebergs were blue,
And the bryum moss and braya herb grew.
The first gift, when blown, always brought aid,
And the other healed wounds, however made.

Then, one blessed day late in the spring,
Runners brought news to the Queen and King
That caused celebrations to begin,
And spread throughout the Kingdom of Klyn,
Tidings of a princess that had been born
To Aleah and Khalen that very morn.

They named the princess, Rhodora Rose,
For the blooms that grew 'round the porticos
Of the Palace of Klyn for untold years
Like faithful floral courtiers.
From realm to realm the tidings passed,
Till they reached the Wanton's ear at last.

And he, whose manner was ever vile,
And whose temper at best took little to rile,
Became enraged at the joys of Klyn,
And vowed to wreak havoc on all its kin.
He swore dire vengeance on Khalen of Klyn,
Who did the hand of Aleah win.

Just what transpired and the part he played
Ere the wages of sin were finally paid,
Is a tale upon other pages writ,
And there you must go to read of it.
It tells why the wasted Barrens lie
Beneath fair Terra Nova's sky,
Where, once, there stood the Kingdom of Klyn,
In every world, a world within.

THE CHILDREN OF KLYN

All of a summer's evening,
Late in the month of June,
When the only light is the lunar light
Of a moon robed in midnight noon,
Softly, from the mountain's height
Down to the moors, the sea,
Is heard the echo of voices bright,
Long vanished, long lost to me.

Only on such nights as these,
When the world seems serene and sure,
Can be heard the voices, through the trees,
Of the children of Klyn, so pure.

Youthful souls of a noble realm,
At home on mountain and moor,
Whose tale cannot but overwhelm,
The children of Klyn, so pure.

For 'twas on a night like this,
Ages and ages past,
That the Wasting Wanton's demon hiss
First vented its fearsome blast!

Aye, 'twas on a night, a night like this,
As the innocents slumbered in dreamy bliss
That their parents saw them last.
For, as they slept in cradle and bed,
The Wasting Wanton came,
And over each trusting childish head.
He uttered his words of shame,
"Tonight, my revenge, just as I swore,
For all men have done to me!

From this time forth, forevermore,
Klyn's children shall flowers be!
No more to drink from cups and bowls,
No more to kneel at mother's knee.
Tonight, the Wanton shall steal their souls!

The children of Klyn shall flowers be!
Iris, laurel, and buttercup,
Clover, and mayflower bloom.
Come, bluebell, and daisy springing up,
Souls enchanted in floral doom!"

And so it was, the very next morn,
Not a child was to be found.
But near the towns whence they were born,
New wildflowers all around!
Nor should their parents ever have known
Just what the fiend had done,
Had not the deed in a vison been shown
To the King of Klyn's own son.

Prince Khalen vowed a vow that day,
To seek out and find the Devil's churl,
And in righteous vengeance make him pay
For the soul of each boy and girl!

How that happened, and what he did,
Are written in another place,
How ended the Prince's royal quest,
How those two met face to face!

Evening and morn are another day,
And time brought new babes to Klyn,
And strangers who passed would nod and say,
"In every world, a world within!"

BIOGRAPHY
OF
D. VAUGHN HARBIN

D. Vaughn Harbin was born Friday, May 13, 1955 at Grace Memorial Hospital, St. John's, Newfoundland, Canada, to parents, Victor George Harbin (businessman) and Alma B. (Laite) Harbin (teacher). The family moved from their home in St. John's to Stephenville on Newfoundland's West Coast in 1957, and remained there until 1968. In that year, they moved to Grand Falls (now Grand Falls- Windsor) in Central Newfoundland, where Vaughn graduated from F. G. Bursey Memorial Collegiate in June 1972

In September 1972, at age 17, he began his pursuit of higher education, which would take him, eventually, to twelve colleges and universities in Canada, the United States and France. He served as an assistant minister in a church in Springdale, Newfoundland for eight months before beginning a thirty-year career as a teacher in various schools across the Island of Newfoundland and in Montreal, Quebec.

He retired from teaching in 2009, and currently lives in Brampton, Ontario, Canada near most of his siblings. He continues to work as a poet, editor, and lyricist.

www.keyclefproduction.com/vaughn-harbin